THE
SITUATION
ROOM

J. G. BROWN

ISBN: Paperback   978-1-952750-22-9

CONTENTS

INTRODUCTION

T he Situation Room title has been made most famous in America's capital Washington D. C., as being known for the President of the United States and its cabinet members and military generals to meet specifically in a specially designated, and specially designed room.

In this inspirational writing, I will paraphrase this room as a metaphor to an even more important room that has similarities to the Washington D.C. set up. The script in its design is meant only to inspire, arrest, and engage one's mind, spirit and soul into an arena not common to life's daily menu.

The information you're about to read is not familiar to most people, but I'm about to share a secret with you from God, the creator of the heavens and earth.

But first, I want to share some of the details of the White House situation room. I'll be paraphrasing some points in revealing (God's situation room), and who is commissioned to be chosen as cabinet, military strategist, and advisors in the room.

The White House situation room is filtrated with extremely highly technical devices, specifically designed conference table, inner and outer chairs positioned for strategic thinking with the themes and seating underline construction of high levels of stress.

Communication devices just short of communicating with heaven, during identified possible military maneuvers international and national security threats.

These threats can range from economic, health and drug epidemics, surges of violence foreign and domestic, and many more. Ultimately, they require the attention of governmental response for the safety and welfare of all people.

The people in the room have been commissioned by the president after much investigation into their career and academic achievement to lead specific departments within the sitting white house administration to be its chief administrator and trusted with the most serious information.

The high level of security clearences are critical and partially based on their history of ability to bring above the rim professional experience, qualifications, and ability to contribute exceptional quality advice and over-opinionated compulsive analysis in the most extreme crisis.

This out of the box posture is great, the conflict often in the room sometime presses the birth of resolution that can lead to unprecedented genius, contribution and maybe even offer complete formulas of resolution to the elephant in the room.

This commission requires in its investigative analysis high levels of security clearance from agencies within the government that specialize in obtaining hidden secrets, not even privileged to high levels of military state and national levels of persons who have high security clearances.

This room is designed especially for the Commander-in-chief's specific choices of persons in the room. They are contacted through specific high-level security measures which are designed in creation to never be compromised or breeched.

Once in the situation room the crisis information is briefed the cabinet members, white house staff and military leaders in the room. And then the dialogue begins.

THE CALL

- People whom God call to the situation room are comprised of an unlimited resource of backgrounds in life experience, for example the journey to the situation room is comprised of persons who have had enormous success, responsibilities, and achievement only to be broken by life, made over and reinvented.
- Some have suffered grief and lost without explanation, whose prayers have sometimes been unspoken unrehearsed and sometimes without breath.
- Some are mighty in life, and like the Lion they roar and hunt any invasion and invaders in the earth who defy spiritual faith or any enmity with the will of God in the earth and the human family. These contend for the faith once delivered to themselves any nation, city, town, who name the name of Christ.
- The call comes to those who have previously held high commands in life but lost their commission because of one-mistake that cannot be taken back from people whose positions award them expedience to cause harm, and there prey can only walk away.
- These are those who have taken up the cross and share God's pain for the pains of those he loves, everyone. The situation

room in conjunction with the charge of the commissioned cabinet members, calls to those who were once beloved and were once life's favorites who are suddenly hated, despised, cast out of Egypt, and given a staff to walk the plains of life's desert and have been left to talk to God in dry places on the backside of life's mountain.

- The call is to those who have arrived at no place to go but prayer, and suddenly they are seeing the bush that burns but is not consumed. They submit and cry out, "Lord whom am I that I should be called?"

- The call is to those whose God's affection and consciousness is without measure, their locations vary from hiding in the mountains, caves, and thickets of life, to command post and exposure in the high place.

- Some cast against the rocks by waves of life who can no longer show their faces in public, they've been left alone abandoned and fallen to their knees, because as the 16th President of the United States wrote: "I have found that inevitably I have no were else to go, but to pray."

- To others the call to become a member of the situation room is to those whose dreams have been granted, denied and delayed by divine providence to twist and turn the rudder of the boat of their lives to position their heart, spirit, mind, and body to the place of humility, brokenness, intercession, supplication, conquest, shame, praise, worship and even defeat while being fashioned in the hand of the Potter.

- It comes to those who have been served a warrant for their arrest, and do not resist but go willingly through the booking process and have been tried and convicted as charged, and sentenced to a lifestyle of prayer in the depth, width, height and breath of the Commander in Chief's charge, and yet are exercising freedom between assignments.

MATTHEW 14:22 LEAVE ME ALONE

After performing phenomenal things in people's lives, relieving oppression, healing terminal illnesses, imparting hope, creating an exciting atmosphere of the supernatural suggesting that maybe some things are impossible, but with God, the living God, all things are possible.

Christ issues a bulletin, (I need to be alone) and he takes charge of the next few events that occur by dismissing the multitudes, sending the disciples away, at which point he goes to a place of solitude.

He understood the necessary reality to take time to pray and spend time with God the Father. It would serve our life great success and inner healing, restoration, completeness, fulfillment, to sow into our lives time with God alone.

To begin talking to him, expressing your most inner thoughts, what your feeling, what makes you happy and your thoughts of thankfulness.

Things that are concerning you, preeminent thoughts of things to come, land mark events, repeated cycled events you'd like to break, successes you'd like to experience, what if anything would he want you to pray for that concerns him.

God wants to spend time with you alone, do something bold and brazen, make a life impacting decision and mark your personal calendar a set time to pray. Write down things you would say if you were going to see the King while he sits on the throne, but keep in mind, he is also your Father.

Would you talk to your father formally, probably not, I have two children and just the other day my son eleven said, "Dad can you take me to get something to eat, I don't want what Nana's, making for diner, just me and you, and can we stay there and eat together."

We talked like twin souls wrapped and entwined in life, unremovable. He talked about his class, his school, the teams he plays on, the next iphone he wants, what he wants to achieve, his friends and all this over pizza.

I listened attentively and stayed connected, without interruption with the intention in my own mind to move without his knowledge to make everything within my control to make those things happen. God would love to spend time with you, hear your thoughts, share your dreams, goals, all you need to do is make the appointment informally, just kidding, you never need an appointment, just you and him, anytime is the time.

PRAYERS OF ACKNOWLEDGEMENT

Our life's prayer should be simple at the start, acknowledging the creator, the sovereignty of things you've identified that are evident in your life, that God has been and is present, and your appreciation.

Thus producing prayer of thanks, humbleness before him, and not forgetting to keep in your time management nourishing your relationship with him, by continual prayer and communication.

INVESTMENT PRAYERS

When I was in my early twenties, I worked for a major international bank as a teller in Manhattan. I learned that there were different types of banks, the one I worked for had corporate clients at the retail level where you would go to either a teller or what was called a platform assistant and or the floor manager.

There were tellers just for international currency. There were platform floors in the building just with bank managers whose portfolio were only high end corporate accounts and/or individual persons or groups with a financial portfolio encompassing wealth. This floor was known for wealth management.

I later learned that there was an aspect of the bank that was labeled investment banking this was a floor entirely dedicated to wealthy people and some of the levels range from low hundreds of thousands to 1-million dollars minimum investment counseling.

But this was still way out of the reach of the middle class, subclass, subculture population, working and maybe putting some money away enough to put in an account labled C.D. known as certificate of deposit, Now these were based on smaller amounts and time spans.

You could take $500.00 and put in a C.D. for 90 days 6-months, 1-year or longer and the longer you decide the higher interest percentage on the total amount you deposited would yield.

This is also another type of prayer, when you take time to pray collective at a church group, family setting, or prayer band and also maintain a daily prayer savings and checking account for your daily life

The certificate of deposit can be compared to portions, revenues of time, energy, emotion, and share them for things that are important and necessary at first, but share them with time with the giver of all things.

Investment prayer is valuing the creator beyond the basic plateau of what he offers. Investment prayer is taking your time and pressing into a new place. It is now not only asking God for something, the minimal thanks and praise, and or routine fundamental prayer process.

INTERCESSORY PRAYERS

When something is important enough for you to actually take the place of someone or some cause, social, economic, surges of violence and many more you get in God's face and plead for his input to change the predictable outcome.

- It is praying for more longterm and life measuring items like the future of your families success, people you know facing challenges, endangered youth, and seniors. The quality level of the economy, welfare, health, and public safety within your county, state, and nation.
- The local clinics and hospital's economic, scientific development, quality of employee relations. The natural and spiritual conscious and health of persons unexposed to relationship, with God and people. The mental health of people from all walks, races, economic backround, provinces. For medical interventions which directly channel suicide prevention along with breakthrough therapy in psychiatry research, for the suicide hot line and the 911 operator.
- Pray for your fire, police, correction officers, nurses, maintenance, engineering staff, all persons of every aspect of life's necessities who contribute on the front line, the military enlisted, and their families.

- People who bring their heart to their profession, job, career be separated from the evil intention staff, and those of the dark side be exposed and expelled.

- The foster care system of adults and children, the local food banks, at least (1) other country, state, county, town, village, and neighbor medical emergency response teams.

- Where as prayer itself could be just talking to God about any and everything, thanks, praise, the future, events of the past. Telling him how you feel, making inquiry about things you've prayed for in the past. Pleas of passion, heart breakage, raw exposed valuable places of the heart that voice prayer request to God with pre-conviction that no cannot be an option.

MATTHEW 14TH
CHAPTER THE STORM

C hrist told his disciples to take the next boat going to the other side of the sea, and he would come later. In similar pattern our journey commences, we start our lives in the development stages through infancy, child, adolescence, young adulthood etc.

The journey is to carve out our place in the world through job, vocation, avocation, talents, maybe a professional career, or stay at home mom or dad. Suddenly we're living out our potential and in similarity of going to the other side.

As we live out our life with goals, achievements, or wondering until we find our way, or a specific purpose in life, one way or the other we are in life's journey, or in the boat going to the other side and time is accumulating as we live and journey onward whether we are living our dream, stagnant, passive, merely along for the ride, or challenging every stage of life.

The bible records in the Book of Ecclesiastes, for everything there is a season, time and purpose under the son, as you know there are four seasons, and nothing just stays the same, everyday the sun rises and sets, the earth rotates, and time is forever moving and changing moment by moment.

- By now the disciples are well into their journey, and what normally would have taken not less than the time of a small trip to the grocery store turns out to be one of their life's biggest challenges.
- They set sail and began a simple journey from one side to the other, but as they journeyed the weather changed drastically.
- The temperature dropped, the waves began to be violent, and the winds became boisterous due to sudden storm conditions. It was unusually dark, and the disciples were afraid and wondering whether or not they were going to make it to the other side.

Parallel to our own lives we start our journey and initially (for the most part) things go well and certainly with reasonable expectation we can anticipate the sea of life to change during our journey.

However, when there is no forecast for an impending storm it can catch us by surprise and depending on the category of the storm, we can experience some unthinkable reactions and responses to our life's journey.

For example, just recently we experienced a small snow storm, nothing unusual but the town did not give any warnings of hazardous road conditions, or early school closings resulting in numerous accidents, extreme delays in school bus drop offs. Consequently, residents blasted the local government officials.

- Suddenly waves bigger than the normal ones, now their begining to hit the boat of our life, these waves are higher than others in the past, its caught our attention and some of the backlash bounces so high it overlaps the rails sometimes pouncing our face itself.

- Waves begin to crash against the boat, water overlaping the entire side of the rail and rocks the boat. Perhaps alarming but, having set sail we understood that these were some of the factors or calculated risk when sailing and having lived its not our first sail across the sea from one side to the other.

- But at times the winds can become fierce and often there is no stable place to become secure in the things we've been confident and relied on in the past in the boat of life we are traveling in the present moment.

- For some of us the waves of life can seem relentless, the continuing crashing of one thing after the other. The crashing waves of health challenges, haunting thoughts of the past, indecisiveness and passivity, unfulfilled goals, success without balance.

The seemingly perfect life with an unexplainable emptiness, the title senior citizen at the blink of an eye, longings and emptiness, inner places that are never filled. A slave to habits, trapped in the body you'd trade for another one in a New York minute.

Too young, to old, so close to something and yet so far away, fierce winds that cut through your life's insulation and now here you are, you can't start life over, or go back to the dock or beginning because the boat is to far out in the storm.

Suddenly you find yourself alone, seemingly isolated, even questioning your own sanity as your facing life, and it really doesn't seem like God is anywhere in sight. Even though the captain of the boat has navigational trajectory charts, you seem to be lost in the boat itself.

These waves hunt you down wherever you are in the boat, these waves don't allow comfort, the winds deny business as usual, and just about now the clock indicates it is the 4th, watch of the night. The absolute darkest before the sunrise begins. However, Jesus has begun his journey to keep his promise I will meet you, as he heads towards them, he walks on the water during the storm.

GOD IS LOOKING FOR YOU

God is suggesting that, he is always up to something, sometimes he merely wants to detain your attention for one moment in your life and use what seems to be the most untimely, unexplainable methods to bring you to acceleration, triumph, and conquest in every aspect of your life.

He is targeting candidates and screening them for something bigger than themselves, he is qualifying candidates by causing alarm, discomfort, setbacks, silence, withdrawal, spiritual intimidation, and harassment.

He's prompting some things in you he has deposited that you have not used before, because they have never been alerted to their consciousness.

The parallel and or similarity will be to point out the very significant aspects of the methods in which there is divine interruption, and intervention, during life's best of times, and worst of times that appear bigger than our ability to control and or handle.

- When things are happening simulcast to others at times when you can't see God and question what the darkness on the canvas of your life's painting is.
- God wants to reveal the purpose in the use of the colors of life on the canvas no matter how dark, God uses the darkness on

the canvas of your life when blending the colors in order to bring out the most illuminating brightest designs.

- He wants to put you in a position to do the miraculous, to point out that even in the night seasons of your life he is moving to do something significant.

- The portal for any move, release, blessing, impowerment, spiritual act will always be through prayer, these prayers are not boot camp training prayers, these are prayers on the ground, in the line of fire.

- By now some of the disciples recognized something like an image moving towards them. Some of the disciples thought maybe they're just beginning to lose it and see things, others thought that maybe this is a real spirit.

- As the image came closer, one of the disciple's name Peter recognized the image to be Jesus, and he wanted to be sure, so he began to pray out loud.

- Now this prayer is no business as usual prayer, this prayer begins eyes wide open, it is a direct assault, stuffed with desperation, anxiety, anticipation, faith, excitement, and the phenomenal. For Peter this was the perfect storm, it was a symposium of the right time, energy, frame of mind, spirit, soul, and body.

- For him the waves were signs of triumph and conquest, they cried to him, if not now, if not here, when and where. We are here to stir your soul, Peter, it's your turn and your time to write the next chapter of magnificence for all to know. Peter, come out here with us, step out of your comfort zone.

- If this is Jesus here now walking on the water towards us than things are not what they seem. If its him than things are about to change, and Peter wants a piece of the action. Peter senses this is the day, something is in the air, the atmosphere, somehow, he knows nothing is ever going to be the same again.

There is a volcanic movement in the inner person, fire is burning, life is boiling because he senses that his God is moving toward him, and he can't be still. He could give attention to the elements, quiver and stay in his pain, fear, anxiety, and circumstances. But if this is really God here and now than this is divine intervention, divine interruption and anything is possible right here, right now in his inner person, lived out through his outer person.

Peter immediately recognizes this moment as a signal from God himself, this is the situation room prayer moment. Peter responds with roaring prayers, lined with ferocious attitude, dreams, desires of a lifetime all packaged into one prayer question. (Lord if it's you, allow me to come upon the waters). Peter is really saying: Let me defy the odds and break the cycle of the boat mentality of this chapter in my life.

Same cast, same past, I may never be in this position ever again, Lord is it you, I don't want to make a mistake. Now that I see you the waves are not so big, the winds are not so fierce, I'm ready to live above my circumstances.

Peter understood that what he does right there, right then in the boat would defy the rest of his entire life, his life brand of ministry, expression, writings, life song, and prayer dialogue will all be defined based on this pivotal moment of action. Peter recognized that this is a situation room moment.

For once I have a chance to cease the high seas of life, I can leave the dunghill, and walk among the greats within my own right, finally I can write a screen play, novel, start the prayer group, start my business, live my dreams, break stereotypes, Lord if it's you, call me out so I know that I know.

I want to live miraculous, phenomenal, undefined, unexplainable. I'm ready to make my mark in life. I want to walk on top of the things that were on top of me. As the Lord comes closer, Peter knows now that this is Jesus, and Jesus answers Peter's prayer and says to Peter, (Be of good cheer, it is I, be not afraid, but come). First, look at what Jesus did, he approaches the disciples in the boat by walking on the water to show them that circumstances whatever they are, are not meant to defy you, you are meant to defy them.

They are merely methods God uses to engage you, stretch your faith, prayer life, bring you to the place of (discovery) of who you really are inside, and hidden capabilities. Did you really think that your life's journey was going to just be a boat ride from one side to the other? Business as ususual.

If it's you, call me out to come to you, if it's you than I know that the prayer I'm praying is being heard directly right now by you, if it's you, than all that I am is known by you, if it's you, all is complete, you are here, I don't need to do any spiritual exercises, you are here.

There is nothing known, that is not known by you. I realize that the only thing to do is to be with you. Do I really need to pray, you are here, this is really the ultimate divine reality, bid me to come with you on the waters? Peter recognized divine geography, divine intimacy, prayer in the heights, widths, breaths, was the place to be, with Christ. The situation room does not call everyone, there were 11 other disciples in the boat but only Peter recognized the moment for what it really was beyond the time, the elements of wind, temperature, waves and present company, the hearsay, gossip, and schisms. He made a conscious decision to engage in the moment and pray.

IN THE BOAT

Wow look at this. It's really Christ walking on the water, and Peter is about to take his crazy self off the ledge to go to him. Oh my God, no not me, I'm tired, cold, hungry, and weak, maybe under different circumstances but not today, I just can't do it.

Let him do it, Jesus didn't ask us to come out there, you know he's going to come in the boat and handle this storm anyway, so why do I need to walk on water.

Hey what's going on. It's Peter, he stepped out, what do you mean he stepped out, Peter is walking on the water, where? oh now I see, it's a miracle, wow I wish it was me but I'm in so much pain.

I'm having a hard-enough time as it is just holding on and staying secure in the boat, I'm not trying to get out. I can't hardly stand up in this craziness. I'm going back to my spot and hold on.

I don't want to step out, I'm just beginning to heal from losing my love one and that kind of drama is extra, I just want Jesus to come in the boat already, Yeah, I understand this was too much for me also.

I just didn't expect this to happen, I just want Christ to come in the boat and touch me when he gets inside, I could use that right now.

Well what about you, well since we are talking, Peter seems to think he's better than us anyway, I hope he sinks, that will teach him. What's your thought, stop hating he's one of us.

I wish I had the adventurous spirit Peter has, I could be walking on the water with Jesus right now instead of just watching on the side line, that looks like some adventure, God help me to step out.

I mean this is great, it's one of the greatest things I've ever seen Jesus do, and it would be Peter. How does this happen? Hey man I don't see nobody blocking your way from stepping out, why don't you just do it.

Jesus is just feet away, I don't need to do a thing. Besides, any second, he'll be coming in the boat and talking with us and he'll comfort us all. You'll see, yeah, I think your right lets just chill and wait.

Taking the position of staying in the boat is just as mature of an act of faith, and trust as stepping out of the boat. God designed the experience to raise the bar and challenge your relationship with him, it was never meant to harm you, cause you to be afraid, as a matter of fact God knows that this storm is going to result in strengthening you, stimulate areas that are stagnant, revive old unproductive places in your life right where you are.

The one outward prayer prayed was immediately answered, Lord if it's you, bid me to come, and he said it is I, come. God hears you in the boat of your life when you pray, and answers with an immediate response.

IT'S ME

It's me, the quiet whisper in the night calling you, come talk with me about the things in your day.

It's me, behind the scenes in your life, making things perfect in every way.

It's me, I caused the storm to awake your soul and arouse your heart, to bring you to great things that I want to impart.

It's me, walking the waves so you can see you don't have to be afraid in the storm, come let me show you, you can live above the norm.

It's me, cleansing stains, slowly healing breakages, mending gaps during this long night, because you are precious, so you would eventually see, I am your light.

I've allowed the gushing waters to push away your past inhibitions and all fears, so you could see I'm drying your eyes with all your tears.

It's me, I allowed the wind to shake your foundations, and the waves to rock the boat you are in, to force you to let go, and just trust me whatever boat you are in.

It's me, you may not see or thank me now, but before this long night is over, your soul will say, "wow".

It's me, just when you thought it was hopeless and this storm of life would never end, it's me walking toward you, saying come and all this will end, walk with me above the waves, despite the temperatures rise and fall, the winds cutting edges, have no affect on me at all.

It's me, I am here right now in every phase of your life, in every breath that you take, every place that you go, I'm walking towards you so you can see and know, be of good cheer, I don't want you to ever be sad, I'm walking in the storm towards you so you can live and be glad.

THE WALK

And Peter climbed down out of the boat and walked on the water towards Jesus, and when he saw the wind boisterous, he was afraid, and beginning to sink he cried, "Lord save me."

And immediately Jesus stretched forth his hand, and caught him, and said unto him, oh thou of little faith, where did thou doubt? And when they climbed into the ship the wind ceased.

Faith, prayer the final frontiers, this was it, something finally came along that was challenging enough, big, small, loud, boisterous, momentous, enough for Peter to climb out of his everyday life and meet who he knew to be the Christ, son of the living God.

This is it, today is the day for you to climb out of the ordinary, routine, and walk with God on the high seas of life, you like Peter, you cannot stay in the boat another minute, it's time, it's your destiny to rewrite the next chapter in your life today, take the step, step out of the boat and walk on the waters.

Walk on the waves of doubt, disease, addiction, poverty, humiliation, self-centeredness, self-absorbedness, pride, loneliness, unfulfillment, self-destruction, worry, fear, broken home, family, age.

Anything that would prevent you from stepping out of the boat you're in and meet Jesus in the place of impossible, triumph, completeness, healing, restoration, reinvention, magnificence, renewal, regeneration, resurgence, resuscitation, and rekindling.

Put your hand in his as you begin to walk the waters of change, new beginnings, trust him through the journey, he has already walked the same waves and he's able to uphold, preserve, sustain, and even carry you to another place in your life full of all the wonders beyond your own imagination.

And when he saw that the wind was contrary, he was afraid and beginning to sink, he cried, "Lord save me." When your faith takes you to the impossible and if you find that the past won't let you go and hunts you down and assaults your faith with a mirage of things to bring you back in the same place you started, pray.

Use what you have, pray, cry out to Jesus and watch what happens, he will always answer immediately when you call in crisis mode, sometimes you will see him deliver with his hand, or something reliably recognizable as his direct hand of deliverance.

But sometimes he orchestrates something in disguise, something untraceable with logic, reasoning, and explanation, he often hides in camouflage of persons, places, impressions, and salvation is delivered directly in the place you never see coming.

THE END GAME

Immediately he reached out his hand, saved him and they both went into the boat and the wind ceased. Faith and prayer are frontiers of necessity, it seemed Peter was the only account of prayer during life's crisis while in the boat. Also, the only record of the act of faith, suggesting that the two go hand and hand.

God is dimensional, he uses mass, length, and time, he always has a set time for something to end that he allowed to enter your life, things you experience are not designed to stay. There is a specific date they arrive, and a specific date they will exit your life.

I like the question he asked, "where did you doubt?" he asked because he thought they connected when he prayed (Lord, if it be thou, bid me to come with you upon the waters), and he said: "Come", and Peter climbed out of the boat and walked with him, but he saw that the winds were contrary, or to say he allowed his inner person to reconnect to the things of the past.

Just prior Peter dismissed the wind, waves, and believed based on his prayer and the immediate answer, come, live, dare to be adventurous, start living your dream, break the status quo, experience success where you are.

If I said you can come with me in this triumphant experience, I certainly have thought out how to get you to the next step. God is never without an exit plan for your challenge, pain, goals, family, finance, romance, children, business, life goal, dreams, desires, illness, life milestones, environment.

In Peter's crisis when he began to sink, Christ immediately reached out his hand and they both went to the boat and the wind ceased. God already had a set time for the wind to cease, the waves to quiet down and the boat to continue the journey to the other side successfully without harm or lost.

But with a renewed measure of faith despite all the things that happen during the process, the doubt, the moments of lost faith, fear, disconnect, worry, gossip, perhaps moments of complete indescribable insanity.

God still walks toward them and causes the wind to diminish, the waves to quiet down and the purposes in their life he intended to be fulfilled. God is for you, loves you, will not leave you in life's storm. You are precious to him, it's your turn and your time, you can step out of your environment.

This specific chapter of your life ends with you triumphant in the storm and making it to the other side of all life's experiences successfully, follow Peter's example, if you find waves dashing, and winds boisterous.

Pray, cry out and he will save you immediately and the wind and waves will cease. God is trying to tell you he's been there all the time when you find yourself praying, Lord is it you, are you in this, and he will answer!

APPLICATION REQUIREMENTS OF THE SITUATION ROOM

- When life's wave's are higher than you've ever imagined
- When winds beat fiercely against your secure places
- When among friends and family, you suddenly sense you're alone and feel afraid
- When your not in charge or control, when you've lost your faith and question what is going on
- When your challenged by uncertainty, even when your challenged by magnificence and the phenomenal
- When you are not accepted, put out, don't belong or fit in unproductive, and productive surroundings with limited and unlimited resources
- When those you love are in danger of living unfulfilled and cut off untimely
- When the time of life has wound up, and your accomplishments don't measure up
- When things are perfect in the splender of all God's best, while at rest in the evening of your life
- When you run to the edges of life's storms, and scream Lord, is it you, there's nothing left, let me come
- When you cannot bear to see another child die, weep until angels from heaven cry, what is your pain?

- When you since creation and the earth itself groaning for all of Gods children to live out their full potential

You are a perfect candidate for the situation room.

INSIDE THE SITUATION ROOM

- First the temperature of the crisis in the room is essential to the navigational trajectory of the meeting in order for the members to at least have one navigational direction, resolution from God.
- Prayers presented in the situation room are unique both in heaven and on earth. They are boisterous, spirited, loud, quiet, out of control, contrite, unrestrained, disorderly, tumultuous, turbulent, unruly, violent, bold, brutal, brutish, cruel in their initial and continuing contingent engagement. After all this is no ordinary room.
- Locations vary but can be considered (amphibious) and or direct assault from prayers by land, air and sea in response to direct ambushes to God's purpose and plan in the earth and lives of those he loves.

God the Commander in Chief has deposited in them his secret, and they have clearance to engage, and contend with violent agitations, lifes tempestuous wind, cyclones, surges that dash against peace, safety, and spiritual stability and the normal decorum and tranquility of life in all of it's stages.

In some instances names and identities are disavowed in order to protect the families of the members of the situation room as well as the members who disguised in order not to be targeted by enemies of the faith who have a form of godliness.

The remaining members identities on the list are kept under the wings of the Almighty. In the situation room the members see the face of him who sees them.

J.G.Brown
Inspirational Speaker / Author

AUTHOR BIO

- Joseph G. Brown is a native of Westchester County N.Y.
- Attended SUNY Sullivan Loch Sheldrake, New York
- Attended Church of Christ Bible College New York, N.Y.
- Law Enforcement Career spans over a decade: Mount Vernon Court Officer, and Ordinance Officer
- General Topics Instructor for New York Cornell Weil University in excess of 15 years
- Supervisor Investigations Unit
- Captain: Department of Public Safety, Monroe Township, N.Y.
- Pastor: Family Church, Saw Creek, Pennsylvania
- *Radio Host: WTHE The Motivational Inspirational Moment*

CERTIFICATIONS

- Crisis Prevention Intervention Instructor
- N.Y. State General Topics Instructor
- John Jay College Investigation
- American Management School, New York, N.Y: *Poised and Powerful Public Speaking*

FAMILY

- Denise Brown, loving and supportive wife. Two children, insightful, athletic son Joseph Jr. and charming, delightful daughter Leah

SPEAKING

- Began speaking engagements as a teenager during junior year in New Rochelle High School. First in churches, youth conferences, and youth services. Began Career at Cornell Weil University, tapped into the broader audience and continued in professional development certifications, and began speaking at other college campuses, youth meetings, community centers, weddings, funerals, and corporate professional development forums, treatment and rehabilitation facilities.

PUBLISHED BOOKS

- The Situation Room, Universal Publishing, 2019; My Father, My Father and Until the Breaking of the Day
- Website: jgbrowninspirationalspeaker.com

CPSIA information can be obtained
at www.ICGtesting.com
Printed in the USA
LVHW091234160921
697947LV00006B/541